Other books by the same author

Poetry

Unit of Five
As Ten As Twenty
The Metal and the Flower
Cry Ararat

Fiction

The Sun and the Moon

p.k. page

Poems Selected and New

Anansi

Some of these poems first appeared in the following maga-
zines: *Ariel, Blackfish, Canadian Forum, Canadian Literature,
Contemporary Verse, First Statement, Outposts, Poetry
Australia, Poetry, Preview, Reading, Tamarack Review.*

Published with the assistance of the Canada Council and the
Ontario Arts Council

Design: Lynn Campbell
Photograph: Nina Raginsky

Typesetting by Annie Buller Typesetting
Printed by The Hunter Rose Company

ISBN: (Paper) 0-88784-031-0 (Cloth) 0-88784-132-5
Library of Congress No.: 74-75921

House of Anansi Press Limited
35 Britain Street
Toronto, Canada

1 2 3 4 5 6   79 78 77 76 75 74

For S.K.

Contents:

IV

I

SUMMER RESORT

They lie on beaches and are proud to tan —
climb banks in search of flowers for their hair,
change colours like chameleons and seem
indolent and somehow flat and sad.

Search out the trees for love, the beach umbrellas,
the bar, the dining-room; flash as they walk,
are pretty-mouthed and careful as they talk;
send picture post-cards to their offices
brittle with ink and soft with daily phrases.

Find Sunday empty without churches — loll
not yet unwound in deck chair and by pool,
cannot do nothing neatly, while in lap,
periscope ready, scan the scene for love.

Under the near leaves or the sailing water
eyes hoist flags and handkerchiefs between the breasts,
        alive,
flutter like pallid bats at the least eddy.

Dread the return which magnifies the want —
wind in high places soaring round the heart
and carried like a star-fish in a pail
through dunes and fields and lonely mountain paths.

But memory, which is thinner than the senses,
is only a wave in grass that the kiss erases,
and love, once found, their metabolism changes:
the kiss is worn like a badge upon the mouth —
pinned there in darkness, emphasized in daylight.

Now all the scene is flying. Before the face
people and trees are swift; the enormous pool
brims like a crying eye. The immediate flesh
is real and night no curtain.

There, together, the swift exchange of badges
accelerates to a personal prize giving
while pulse and leaf rustle and grow climactic.

SHIPBUILDING OFFICE

The strange jargon of ships and their building
floats very lightly, like flotsam
in heads stormily holding the perilous oceans of love.
They are like children at desks,
their farthest eyes tracing
the angle of a first flight,
their nearest ones reading
with uncanny accuracy and no perception
contracts for hawser wire
boilers and cable.

This girl in gingham,
shy as a traitor
her face hardly emerged
from the dive of childhood,
rides the clock with spurs through ship and dock;
unrelated as fable
to nineteen-forty,
her job, her jargon
or the permanent carbon
fixing eight sets of everything angrily upon paper.

OFFICES

Oh believe me, I have known offices —
young and old in them, both —
morning and evening;
felt the air
stamp faces into a mould;
office workers at desks
saying *go* to a typewriter
and *stop* to a cabinet;
taking scrupulous care over calendars
so days
are etched in the outward leaning eyes
while bosses, behind glass like jewels,
are flashing their light and coming suddenly near.

In offices drawers contain
colored paper for copies,
staples, string,
hand lotion and various personal things
like love letters.

In washrooms girls are pretty with their mouths
drawing them fancy; light the sugar-white tube of smoke
and never once question the future, look ahead
beyond payday or ask the *if* that makes them angular.

In elevators, coming and going, they are glib —
tongued and perky as birds with the elevator men.
Some, beautiful and colored always, like singing,
never become the permanent collection
and some — if you speak to them of a different world,
a future more like life — become sharp,
give you their whittled face
and turn away like offended starlings from a wind.

TYPISTS

They without message, having read
the running words on their machines,
know every letter as a stamp
cutting the stencils of their ears.
Deep in their hands, like pianists,
all longing gropes and moves, is trapped
behind the tensile gloves of skin.

Or blind, sit with their faces locked
away from work. Their varied eyes
are stiff as everlasting flowers.
While fingers on a different plane
perform the automatic act
as questions grope along the dark
and twisting corridors of brain.

Crowded together typists touch
softly as ducks and seem to sense
each others' anguish with the swift
sympathy of the deaf and dumb.

PREDICTION WITHOUT CRYSTAL

Oh you girls, with your sad eyes and your visions
of fortune-tellers floating in the pond of the crystal
or breathing on your palms in the electric
moment of seeing marriage written surely,

dreaming the silent room where the gypsied woman
flicks dirty cards by the cluttered paper roses,
juggles with love and conjures up initials —

girls in your leisure hours, awkward at parties,
gaming with sugar dice and casting caution
into the cockle-shell of the secret cauldron,

there is no private world, I tell you truly,
no single room for you except the lonely
room of yourselves. I can predict your futures:

bandstand your bacchanals, the blackened alleys
bright for you, cock-crow your reveille
and darkness your desired and nimble dodger;

you'll walk like crow along the winter furrow
wild in a world of day and mean with terror
while hips and cheek-bones squeak and totter narrow

then run from news-reel, strike and strychnine street
into the room of *you* and die in mirrors
for click and close the camera covers lovers.

PRESENTATION

Now most miraculously the most junior clerk
becomes a hero.
Oh, beautiful child
projected suddenly to executive grandeur,
gone up like an angel in the air of good wishes,
the gift and the speeches.

Dry as chalk from your files you come, unfolding.
In the hothouse they have made of their hearts
you flower
and by a double magic, force their flower —
the gift repaid in the symbol of desire.
You have become quite simply glorious.
They by comparison cannot be less.

Oh, lighted by this dream, the office glows
brightly among the double row of desks.
This day shines in their breasts like emeralds,
their faces wake from sleeping as you smile.
They have achieved new grace because you leave.
Each, at this moment, has a home, has love.

BANK STRIKE

Quebec — 1942

When the time came,
after the historied waiting,
they were ready with their strikers' jackets
and their painted signs "en grève,"
facing the known streets
and the rough serge knees and elbows
of police.

Time was bald on their skins,
their desks and counters and cages
cried in their eyes like a strategical retreat
and the unrelieved picket line
had a stained, for-all-time permanence
on the distorted street.

In the foreground church
the flames of the sacred candles
burned, in their suddenly foreign homes
their meals were stiff as religious paintings
and the bullet of "fired"
was wedged in their skulls.

Yet from the cellar of certainty they came
up the long escalator to defeat,
their hearts hurting their ribs, their hands heavy;
blew hot and cold
and scratched the solid curb
like weather worrying an iron city.

THE INARTICULATE

Dumb are their tongues and doubtful their belief.
And grown too slow to speak,
grow double dumb,
misers of words and miserable when wrapped
tight in a sentence.
(O move the comma half an inch for head
to slip and wriggle through —
the final latch
clicks with the word of sense.)

I see them daily, inarticulate,
on streetcar and on street;
work at their desks
and worm my hearing underneath their skulls,
die from the silence rooted in their tongues,
slide like a cup upon their screaming eyes
and feel the sirens blowing in their necks
vibrate too high for sound.

They wither, tuned for sound, who cannot speak,
hammer all day at keys that do not print,
and file their voices in the teeming vault.
Learning the language of the deaf and dumb
their prayers are lit, but studying fingers creak.
Like foreign papers, no one reads their hands.

OUTCASTS

Subjects of bawdy jokes and by the police
treated as criminals, these lovers dwell
deep in their steep albino love —
a tropic area where nothing grows.

Nobody's brothers, they revolve
on rims of the family circle, seek some place
where nothing shuns them, where no face
in greeting dons the starched immaculate mask.

Look, in their isolation they become
almost devoid of bones, their ward is one
nobody enters, but their least
window requires a curtain. They are clowns

without a private dressing room, with only
one ancient joke to crack now and forever.
They draw a crowd as if they had a band:
Always the healthy are their audiences.

The youths who hunt in packs, bitches with cash,
crafty embezzelers of the public purse,
perjurers and fashionable quacks
slumming, but saintly, saintly, judge them as

outcasts. In the laundered mind they rate
the bottom of the scale, below the Jew
with his hundred hands and pockets and below
niggers whose love is lewd.

Let doctors show a white asceptic hand
within their sickroom and let parents gaze
back against time's tight fist to find the cause —
seek in the child the answer to the man:

search out the early misfit, who at school,
sickly for love and giddy with his sex
found friendship like a door banged in his face,
his world a wasteland and himself a fool.

THE CONDEMNED
(For L.O.)

In separate cells they tapped the forbidden message.
Even the wide-eared warden could never hear
their miniature conversation
though he slipped the bolt of his hearing and walked the
      passage.

Then feeling the walls would dissolve with love they
      planned
the inevitable and leisurely excavation;
tap grew into chip behind the bed
as darkness hid the activities of the hand.

In an area a cigarette could light, everything lived.
The intricate machinery of the head
stopped and the heart's attention
increased the circumference of what they loved.

Then as the wall grew thin they wore their hopes
inwardly like a name they must never mention;
the riots of the skin were still to listen
for the warden's silent black-and-white approach.

And as their fingers groped and came together
it was so suddenly tender in that prison
birds might have sung from water — just as if
two mouths meeting and melting had become each other.

Later the whole hand grasped and the ultimate escape
plunging through velvet to an earth so stiff
their footfall left no mark
though their feet felt sharp, resuming use and shape.

Their lungs, in all that air, filled like balloons,
pastel and luminous against the dark:
no angels could have had more grace
in a children's heaven full of suns and moons.

But light destroyed their splendour, all their soft
movements jerked to woodcuts and the lace
of their imagination atrophied.
Their stark identities — all they had left —

were mirrored upon fence and parish hall
and plastered on the staring countryside
till each became a terror and a face
and everywhere they went was nowhere at all.

MORNING, NOON AND NIGHT

The season of self-pity and of flowers
is here again —
the fine-boned perilous girls
are sprigged with little bows
oh hey ho nonny.

From their moist sleep arising they are great
areas of hot skin and of heart;
trot and clip to work like ponies nobbed
with coloured bow and bobbin for the show —
their hair in manes
and shaggy on their shins.

Dropped from some great height they flop at noon
liquid and lazy with the heat upon
the bright green grass beneath the trees, between
the grey of public stone;
and hardly know their wish
and hardly guess
themselves as more than surface indolence.

Become at night like spikenard and stress
under the hunter's green of hanging leaves;
among the flowering street lamps they are white
and wildly wandering and light
lances their pale and simple eyes.
                                        They move
caught up in eddying water —
they are slow
and urgent and unknowable as moons.

THE STENOGRAPHERS

After the brief bivouac of Sunday,
their eyes, in the forced march of Monday to Saturday,
hoist the white flag, flutter in the snow-storm of paper,
haul it down and crack in the mid-sun of temper.

In the pause between the first draft and the carbon
they glimpse the smooth hours when they were children —
the ride in the ice-cart, the ice-man's name,
the end of the route and the long walk home;

remember the sea where floats at high tide
were sea marrows growing on the scatter-green vine
or spools of grey toffee, or wasps' nests on water;
remember the sand and the leaves of the country.

Bell rings and they go and the voice draws their pencil
like a sled across snow; when its runners are frozen
rope snaps and the voice then is pulling no burden
but runs like a dog on the winter of paper.

Their climates are winter and summer — no wind
for the kites of their hearts — no wind for a flight;
a breeze at the most, to tumble them over
and leave them like rubbish — the boy-friends of blood.

In the inch of the noon as they move they are stagnant.
The terrible calm of the noon is their anguish;
the lip of the counter, the shapes of the straws
like icicles breaking their tongues, are invaders.

Their beds are their oceans — salt water of weeping
the waves that they know — the tide before sleep;
and fighting to drown they assemble their sheep
in columns and watch them leap desks for their fences

and stare at them with their own mirror-worn faces.

In the felt of the morning the calico-minded,
sufficiently starched, insert papers, hit keys,
efficient and sure as their adding machines;
yet they weep in the vault, they are taut as net curtains
stretched upon frames. In their eyes I have seen
the pin men of madness in marathon trim
race round the track of the stadium pupil.

ELECTION DAY

I

I shut the careful door of my room and leave
letters, photographs and the growing poem —
the locked zone of my tight and personal thought
slough off — recede from down the green of the street.
Naked almost among the trees and wet —
a strike for lightning.

And everything rushes at me either fierce or friendly
in a sudden world of bulls.
Faces on posters in the leaves call out
the violent yes or no to my belief.
Are quick or slow or halted to my pulse.

Oh on this beautiful day, the weather wooing
the senses and the feel of walking
smooth in my summer legs
I lope through the tall and trembling grass and call
the streaming banner of my public colour.

II

Here in this place, the box and private privet
denote the gentleman and shut him in —
for feudally he lives and the feud on.
Colonel Evensby with his narrow feet
will cast his blue blood ballot for the Tory.

And in the polling station I shall meet
the smiling rather gentle overlords
propped by their dames and almost twins in tweeds
and mark my x against them and observe
my ballot slip, a bounder, in the box.

And take my route again through lazy streets
alive with all-out blossoming, through trees
that stint no colour for their early summer
and past an empty lot where an old dog
appoints himself as guardian of the green.

III

Radio owns my room as the day ends.
The slow returns begin, the voices call
the yes's and the no's that ring or toll;
the districts all proclaim themselves in turn
and public is my room, not personal.

Midnight. I wander on the quiet street,
its green swamped by the dark; a pale glow
sifts from the distant lamps. Behind the leaves
the faces on the posters wait and blow
tattered a little and less urgent now.

I pass the empty lot. The old dog
has trotted off to bed. The neighbourhood
is neatly hedged with privet still, the lights
are blinking off in the enormous homes.
Gentlemen, for the moment, you may sleep.

SOME THERE ARE FEARLESS

In streets where pleasure grins
and the bowing waiter
turns double somersaults to the table for two
and the music of the violin is a splinter
pricking the poultice of flesh; where glinting glass
shakes with falsetto laughter,
Fear, the habitué, ignores the menu
and plays with the finger bowl at his permanent table.

Tune in the ear: in tub, in tube, in cloister
he is the villain; underneath the bed,
bare-shanked and shaking; drunken in pubs; or teaching
geography to half a world of children.

In times like these, in streets like these, in alleys,
he is the master and they run for shelter
like ants to ant hills when he lifts his rattle.
While dreaming wishful dreams that will be real,
some there are, fearless, touching a distant thing —
the ferreting sun, the enveloping shade, the attainable spring,
and the wonderful soil, nameless, beneath their feet.

CULLEN

Cullen renounced his cradle at fifteen,
set the thing rocking with his vanishing foot
hoping the artifice would lessen the shock.
His feet were tender as puff-balls on the stones.

He explored the schools first and didn't understand
the factory-made goods they stuffed in his mind
or why the gramaphone voice always ran down
before it reached the chorus of its song.
Corridors led 'from' but never 'to',
stairs were merely an optical illusion,
in the damp basement where they hung their coats
he cried with anger and was called a coward.
He didn't understand why they were taught
life was good by faces that said it was not.
He discovered early 'the writing on the wall'
was dirty words scrawled in the shadowy hall.

Cullen wrote a note on his plate with the yolk of his egg
saying he hardly expected to come back,
and then, closing his text-books quietly
he took his personal legs into the city.
Toured stores and saw the rats beneath the counters
(he visited the smartest shopping centres)
saw the worm's bald head rise in clerks' eyes
and metal lips spew out fantasies.
Heard the time clock's tune and the wage's pardon,
saw dust in the store-room swimming towards the light
in the enormous empty store at night;
young heads fingering figures and floating freights
from hell to hell with no margin for mistakes.

Cullen bent his eye and paid a price
to sit on the mountain of seats like edelweiss —

watched the play pivot, discovered his escape
and with the final curtain went backstage;
found age and sorrow were an application,
beauty a mirage, fragrance fictionary,
the ball dress crumpled, sticky with grease and sweat.
He forgot to close the stage door as he went.

He ploughed the city, caught on a neon sign,
heard the noise of machines talking to pulp,
found the press treacherous as a mountain climb:
all upper case required an alpenstock.
Tried out the seasons then, found April cruel —
there had been no Eliot in his books at school —
discovered that stitch of knowledge on his own
remembering all the springs he had never known.
Summer grew foliage to hide the scar,
bore leaves that looked as light as tissue paper
leaves that weighed as heavy as a plate.
Fall played a flute and stuck it in his ear,
Christmas short-circuited and fired a tree
with lights and baubles; hid behind Christ; unseen
counted its presents on an adding-machine.

Cullen renounced the city, nor did he bother
to leave his door ajar for his return;
found his feet willing and strangely slipping like adders
away from the dreadful town.
Decided country, which he had never seen
was carillon greenness lying behind the eyes
and ringing the soft warm flesh behind the knees;
decided that country people were big and free.
Found himself lodgings with fishermen on a cliff,
slung his hammock from these beliefs and slept.
Morning caught his throat when he watched the men

return at dawn like silver-armored Vikings
to women malleable as rising bread.
At last, the environment was to his liking.
Sea was his mirror and he saw himself
twisted as rope and fretted with the ripples;
concluded quietness would comb him out:
for once, the future managed to be simple.

He floated a day in stillness, felt the grass
grow in his arable body, felt the gulls
trace the tributaries of his heart and pass
over his river beds from feet to skull.
He settled with evening like a softening land
withdrew his chair from the sun the oil lamp made,
content to rest within his personal shade.
The women, gathering, tatted with their tongues
shrouds for their absent neighbours and the men
fired with lemon extract and boot-legged rum
suddenly grew immense.
No room could hold them — he was overrun,
trampled by giants, his grass was beaten down.
Nor could his hammock bear him for it hung
limp from a single nail, salty as kelp.

Cullen evacuated overnight,
he knew no other region to explore;
discovered it was nineteen thirty-nine
and volunteered at once and went to war
wondering what on earth he was fighting for.
He knew there was a reason but couldn't find it
and marched to battle half an inch behind it.

POEM IN WAR TIME

Let us by paradox
choose a Catholic close
for innocence,
wince at the smell
of beaded flowers
like rosaries on a bush.
Let us stand together then
till the cool evening
settles this silent place
and having seen the hatted priest
walk with book from presbytery to border
and the pale nuns, handless as seals,
move in the still shadow,
let us stand here close,
for death is common as grass beyond an ocean
and, with all Europe pricking in our eyes,
suddenly remember Guernica
and be gone.

UNABLE TO HATE OR LOVE

In sight of land, everything came at him sharp and bright —
gulls suddener and a higher light on the wave.
New seeing made him a stranger to himself
and now, no longer one of the boys, he was quite alone
and lost in the larger body he had grown
during the sea trip; found himself shy
even with friends and nervous about the soil.

When the carrier came to dock he stood on deck
close-pressed among the rest. From the waiting bus
there to despatch him to a camp, he was
identical with the others — a khaki boy
released to freedom, returning from the East.
And though he had longed for freedom, found it hard
to visualize the walk along the street
or conversing with a girl
or the girl's speech.

It was almost as if there were figures behind his eyes
that he couldn't completely see around or through;
as if in front of him there were others who
partially blocked his view, who might even speak
gibberish or cry if he opened his mouth.

He wished, for the moment, he needn't go ashore
into this unknown city of friends. Already
the mayor had welcomed them by radio,
the sirens that hooted and screamed had made him a fool,
the people lining the docks were weeping for him
and everywhere hankies and flags fluttered but he
came from unnamed country.

Three years he had dreamed this moment and how, running
he would tear with his smile the texture of this air;

he had dreamed that peace could instantly replace war.
But now he was home and about to land and he feared
the too-big spaces and the too-blue skies
and knew, at last, that most of his dreams were lies
and himself a prisoner still behind his face,
unable to be free in any place;
to hate the enemy as they wished him to
or love his countrymen as he would like to do.

GENERATION

Schooled in the rubber bath,
promoted to scooter
early, to evade and dart;
learning our numbers
adequately, with a rivetting tongue;
freed from the muddle of sex
by the never-mention method
and treading
the treacherous tight-rope
of unbelieved religion,
we reached the dreadful
opacity of adolescence.

We were an ignored
and undeclared ultimatum
of solid children;
moving behind our flesh
like tumblers on the lawn
of an unknown future,
taking no definite shape —
shifting and merging
with an agenda
of unanswerable questions
growing like roots.

Tragically, Spain was our spade;
we dug at night;
the flares went up in the garden.
Walking down country lanes
we committed arson —
firing our parent-pasts;
on the wooded lands
our childhood games grew real:

police and robbers
held unsmiling faces
against each other.

We strapped our hands in slings
fearing the dreaded
gesture of compromise;
became a war;
knew love roll from a bolt
long as the soil
and, loving, saw
eyes like our own
studding the map like cities.

Now we touch continents
with our little fingers,
swim distant seas
and walk on foreign streets
wearing crash helmets
of permanent beliefs.

WAR LORD IN THE EARLY EVENING

Suitable for a gentleman with medals
to choose for pleasure
and his beneficent care
the long-stemmed roses wilting in the summer weather.

Fitting for a man in his position
to succour them with water
at his side
admiring, dressed in muslin, his small daughter.

He saw the picture clearly. It was charming:
the battered war lord
in the early evening
among the roses, gentle and disarming.

The way he sent the servants for the hoses
they thought a fire was raging
in the garden.
Meanwhile the roses and the light were fading.

Six choppy lengths of tubing were assembled.
Bind them, the general stormed
from six make one.
Was this philosophy? It wasn't plumbing.

How bind six hoses of assorted sizes
all minus fixtures?
Though his servants shrugged
they dropped to a man on their knees and bound their fingers

tightly around the joints and five small fountains
gushed at specific places
on the lawn
and cooled five straining servants' sweating faces.

Pitiful the little thread of water
that trickle, that distil.
The darkness hid
a general toying with a broken water pistol.

Hid from his daughter, frail organza issue
of his now failing loin
the battle done:
so much militia routed in the man.

Sic transit gloria mundi. I would rather
a different finish.
It was devilish
that the devil denied him that one innocent wish.

WAKING

I lie in the long parenthesis of arms
dreaming of love
and the crying cities of Europe

wake to the bird a whistler in my room
and sun a secret

Light on the bed of air
and bouyed by morning
the easy bugle of breath
projects an echo

while over the difficult room
the brimming window
opens the bandaged eyes
to the shape of Asia.

Invalid, I —
and crippled by sleep's illness,
drowned in the milk of sheets
and silk of dreams,
I rise and write the upward curve of day
with mercury of the smashed thermometer
and trouble the silent mirror, who have been
pale in suspension on the oval bed.

ISOLATIONIST

When the many move, the man
in the cubicle of content
cowers, suddenly discovered, suddenly rent
by the reality of crowds.
He has trained the climbing vine,
written "roses" on his ledger,
lived like a saint and finds himself a leper.

Immaculate of belief and violent on Mondays,
thinking no evil and thanking no second party
he has leaned in the evenings on the low-lipped window
and learned of his saintliness from outlines of lovers.

Now lovers leap the sash and the many winnow
his penny bank of wisdom and set it swirling
down the unclogged drain in the hidden scullery.
People take solid shape and are vividly human,
smash walls, uproot chairs and juggle cutlery
while he sits with gloved hands in a buttoned confusion.

AS TEN AS TWENTY

For we can live now, love:
a million in us breathe,
moving as we move
and qualifying death

in lands our own and theirs
with simple hands as these
a walk as like as hers
and words as like as his.

They in us free our love
make archways of our mouths,
tear off the patent gloves
and atrophy our myths.

As ten, as twenty, now
we break from single thought
and rid of being two
receive them and walk out.

II

THE LANDLADY

Through sepia air the boarders come and go,
impersonal as trains. Pass silently
the craving silence swallowing her speech;
click doors like shutters on her camera eye.

Because of her their lives become exact:
their entrances and exits are designed;
phone calls are cryptic. Oh, her ticklish ears
advance and fall back stunned.

Nothing is unprepared. They hold the walls
about them as they weep or laugh. Each face
is dialled to zero publicly. She peers
stippled with curious flesh;

pads on the patient landing like a pulse,
unlocks their keyholes with the wire of sight,
searches their rooms for clues when they are out,
pricks when they come home late.

Wonders when they are quiet, jumps when they move,
dreams that they dope or drink, trembles to know
the traffic of their brains, jaywalks their street
in clumsy shoes.

Yet knows them better than their closest friends:
their cupboards and the secrets of their drawers,
their books, their private mail, their photographs
are theirs and hers.

Knows when they wash, how frequently their clothes
go to the cleaners, what they like to eat,
their curvature of health, but even so
is not content.

And like a lover must know all, all, all.
Prays she may catch them unprepared at last
and palm the dreadful riddle of their skulls —
hoping the worst.

ADOLESCENCE

In love they wore themselves in a green embrace.
A silken rain fell through the spring upon them.
In the park she fed the swans and he
whittled nervously with his strange hands.
And white was mixed with all their colours
as if they drew it from the flowering trees.

At night his two-finger whistle brought her down
the waterfall stairs to his shy smile
which, like an eddy, turned her round and round
lazily and slowly so her will
was nowhere — as in dreams things are and aren't.

Strolling along avenues in the dark
street lamps sang like sopranos in their heads
with a violence they never understood
and all their movements when they were together
had no conclusion.

Only leaning into the question had they motion;
after they parted were savage and swift as gulls.
Asking and asking the hostile emptiness
they were as sharp as partly sculptured stone
and all who watched, forgetting, were amazed
to see them form and fade before their eyes.

THE BANDS AND THE BEAUTIFUL CHILDREN

Band makes a tunnel of the open street
at first, hearing it;
seeing it band becomes
high: brasses ascending on the strings of sun
build their own auditorium of light,
windows from cornets
and a dome of drums.

And always attendant on bands, the beautiful children
white with running and innocence;
and the arthritic old
who, patient behind their windows
are no longer split by the quick yellow of imagination
or carried beyond their angular limits of distance.

But the children move
in the trembling building of sound,
sure as a choir
until band breaks and scatters,
crumbles about them and is made of men
tired and grumbling
on the straggling grass.

And the children, lost, lost,
in an open space,
remember the certainty of the anchored home
and cry on the unknown edge of their own city
their lips stiff from an imaginary trumpet.

LITTLE GIRLS

More than discovery — rediscovery.
They renew
acquaintanceship with all things
as with flowers in dreams.

And delicate as a sketch made by being,
they merge in a singular way with their own thoughts,
drawing an arabesque with a spoon or fork
casually on the air behind their shoulders,
or talk in a confidential tone as if
their own ears held the hearing of another.

Legs in the dance go up as though on strings
pulled by their indifferent wanton hands

while anger blows into them and through their muslin
easily as sand or wind.

Older, they become round and hard, demand
shapes that are real, castles on the shore
and all the lines and angles of tradition
are mustered for them in their eagerness
to become whole, fit themselves to the thing
they see outside them,
while the thing they left
lies like a caul in some abandoned place,
unremembered by fingers or the incredibly bright
stones, which for a time replace their eyes.

SISTERS

These children split each other open like nuts,
break and crack in the small house,
are doors slamming.
Still, on the whole, are gentle for mother, take
her simple comfort like a drink of milk.

Fierce on the street they own the sun and spin
on separate axes
attract about them in their motion all
the shrieking neighbourhood of little earths,
in violence hold hatred in their mouths.

With evening their joint gentle laughter leads
them into pastures of each others eyes;
beyond, the world is barren; they contract
tenderness from each other like disease
and talk as if each word had just been born —
a butterfly, and soft from its cocoon.

YOUNG GIRLS

Nothing, not even fear of punishment
can stop the giggle in a girl.
Oh mothers' trim
shapes on the chesterfield cannot dispel
their lolloping fatness.
Adolescence tumbles about in them
on cinder schoolyard or behind the expensive gates.

See them in class like porpoises
with smiles and tears
loosed from the same subterranean faucet; some
find individual adventure in
the obtuse angle, some in a phrase
that leaps like a smaller fish from a sea of words.
But most, deep in their daze, dawdle and roll,
their little breasts like wounds beneath their clothes.

A shoal of them in a room makes it a pool.
How can one teacher keep the water out,
or, being adult, find the springs and taps
of their tempers and tortures?
Who on a field filled with their female cries
can reel them in on a line of words
or land them neatly in a net?
On the dry ground they goggle, flounder, flap.

Too much weeping in them and unfamiliar blood
has set them perilously afloat.
Not divers these — but as if the waters rose in flood —
making them partially amphibious
and always drowning a little and hearing bells;
until the day the shore line wavers less,
and caught and swung on the bright hooks of their sex,
earth becomes home, their natural element.

BLOWING BOY

He is, I think, somebody else and not this
flapping and swaying apparition on strings.
Even his eyes are newly painted and not his
and I have seen his hands like a pair of old gloves
that are hungry for hands, hanging with only air
bulging the fingertips.

World is a wind about him. Everything blows.
Objects rise up and fly away like crows,
become small specks or nothing — cease to exist.
Within him there
seems to be no ballast against this air.
He spins out on a long string grown tight
and splits an acre of blue sky like a kite.

Night laps about him. In the liquid dark
all his words are released and new words find him.
Like homing pigeons come his blowing thoughts
back to roost within him. He is huge —
the burning centre of
everything, but most especially love.

Waking from dreams sometimes he is a ship
without the crew or chart to master it.
He is half master, half his master's fool
but on the corner with the boys his laugh
can halve a passing girl and make him whole.

PARANOID

He loved himself too much. As a child was god.
Thunder stemmed from his whims,
flowers were his path.
Throughout those early days his mother was all love,
a warm projection of him
like a second heart.

In adolescence, dark and silent, he was perfect;
still godlike and like a god
cast the world out.
Crouching in his own torso as in a chapel
the stained glass of his blood
glowed in the light.

Remained a god. Each year he grew more holy
and more wholly himself.
The self spun
thinner and thinner like a moon forming
slowly from that other self
the dead sun.

Until he was alone, revolved in ether
light years from the world,
cold and remote.
Thinking he owned the heavens too, he circled,
wanly he turned and whirled
reflecting light.

ONLY CHILD

The early conflict made him pale
and when he woke from those long weeping slumbers she was
                                                          there
and the air about them — hers and his —
sometimes a comfort to him, like a quilt, but more
often than not a fear.

There were times he went away — he knew not where —
over the fields or scuffing to the shore;
suffered her eagerness on his return
for news of him — where had he been, what done?
He hardly knew, nor did he wish to know
or think about it vocally or share
his private world with her.

Then they would plan another walk, a long
adventure in the country, for her sake —
in search of birds. Perhaps they'd find the blue
heron today, for sure the kittiwake.

Birds were familiar to him now, he knew
them by their feathers and a shyness like his own
soft in the silence.
Of the ducks she said, "Observe,
the canvas back's a diver," and her words
stuccoed the slatey water of the lake.

He had no wish to separate them in groups
or learn the latin,
or, waking early to their song remark, "the thrush,"
or say at evening when the air is streaked
with certain swerving flying,
"Ah, the swifts."

Birds were his element like air and not
her words for them — making them statues
setting them apart,
nor were they facts and details like a book.
When she said, "Look!"
he let his eyeballs harden
and when two came and nested in the garden
he felt their softness, gentle, near his heart.

She gave him pictures which he avoided, showing
strange species flat against a foreign land.
Rather would he lie in the grass, the deep grass of the island
close to the gulls' nests knowing
these things he loved and needed near his hand,
untouched and hardly seen but deeply understood.
Or sail among them through a wet wind feeling
their wings within his blood.

Like every mother's boy he loved and hated
smudging the future photograph she had,
yet struggled within the frames of her eyes and then
froze for her, the noted naturalist —
her very affectionate and famous son.
But when most surely in her grasp, his smile
darting and enfolding her, his words:
"Without my mother's help . . ." the dream occurred.

Dozens of flying things surrounded him
on a green terrace in the sun
and one by one
as if he held caresses in his palm
he caught them all and snapped and wrung their necks
brittle as little sticks.

Then through the bald, unfeathered air
and coldly as a man would walk
against a metal backdrop, he
bore down on her
and placed them in her wide maternal lap
and accurately said their names aloud:
woodpecker, sparrow, meadowlark, nuthatch.

THE KNITTERS
(for Alice and Sheila)

These women knitting knit a kind of mist —
climate of labyrinth —
into the air.
Sitting like sleepers,
propped against the chintz,
pin-headed somehow — figures by Moore —
arachnes in their webs, they barely stir —

except their eyes and hands, which wired to some
urgent personal circuit,
move as if
a switch controlled them.
Hear the click and hum
as their machines translating hieroglyphs,
compulsive and monotonous, consume —
lozenge and hank — the candy-coloured stuff.

See two observe the ceremony of skeins:
one, forearms raised,
the loops around her palms,
catscradle rocks, is metronome, becalmed;
while her companion
spun from her as from
a wooden spindle, winds a woollen world.

A man rings like an axe, is alien,
imperilled by them,
finds them cold and far.
They count their stitches on a female star
and speak another language,
are not kin.
Or is he Theseus remembering
that maze, those daedal ways, the Minotaur?

49

They knit him out, the wool grows thick and fills
the room they sit in like a fur
as vegetable more than animal,
surrealist and slightly sinister,
driven by motors strong beyond their wills,
these milky plants devour
more hanks of wool, more cubic feet of air.

PORTRAIT OF MARINA

Far out the sea has never moved. It is
Prussian forever, rough as teazled wool
some antique skipper worked into a frame
to bear his lost four-master.
                          Where it hangs
now in a sunny parlour, none recalls
how all his stitches, interspersed with oaths
had made his one pale spinster daughter grow
transparent with migraines — and how his call
fretted her more than waves.
                          Her name
Marina, for his youthful wish —
boomed at the font of that small salty church
where sailors lurched like drunkards, would, he felt
make her a water woman, rich with bells.
To her the name Marina simply meant
he held his furious needle for her thin
fingers to thread again with more blue wool
to sew the ocean of his memory.
Now, where the picture hangs, a dimity
young inland housewife with inherited
clocks under bells and ostrich eggs on shelves
pours amber tea in small rice china cups
and reconstructs
how great-great-grandpapa at ninety-three
his fingers knotted with arthritis, his
old eyes grown agatey with cataracts
became as docile as a child again —
that fearful salty man —
and sat, wrapped round in faded paisley shawls
gently embroidering.

While Aunt Marina in grey worsted, warped
without a smack of salt, came to his call
the sole survivor of his last shipwreck.

* * *

Slightly off shore it glints. Each wave is capped
with broken mirrors. Like Marina's head
the glinting of these waves.
She walked forever antlered with migraines
her pain forever putting forth new shoots
until her strange unlovely head became
a kind of candelabra — delicate —
where all her tears were perilously hung
and caught the light as waves that catch the sun.
The salt upon the panes, the grains of sand
that crunched beneath her heel
her father's voice, "Marina!" — all these broke
her trembling edifice. The needle shook
like ice between her fingers.
In her head
too many mirrors dizzied her and broke.

* * *

But where the wave breaks, where it rises green
turns into gelatine, becomes a glass
simply for seeing stones through, runs across
the coloured shells and pebbles of the shore
and makes an aspic of them
then sucks back
in foam and undertow —
this aspect of the sea

Marina never knew.
For her the sea was Father's Fearful Sea
harsh with sea serpents
winds and drowning men.
For her it held no spiral of a shell
for her descent to dreams,
it held no bells.
And where it moved in shallows it was more
imminently a danger, more alive
than where it lay off shore full fathom five.

CHIMNEY FIRE

Something must be fire for them, these six
brass-helmeted navy-blue navvies come to chop
the old endlessly-polished wainscot with the fireman's axe.
Ready and royal for crisis and climax
shining and stalwart and valiant — for *this?*
Some element in this puny fire must prove
muscled enough for them to pit against,
and so they invade the green room, all six,
square up to its tidy silence and attack.

Only the roar in the brick and that abating
and the place orderly and quiet as a painting
of a house and all their paraphernalia outside waiting
to be used and useless and inside silence growing coolly
as a lily on a green stem.
Oh how they tackle it, hack it, shout it down
only to find it broken out again,
implacably sending up suckers in the still room,
forevergreen, the chill obverse of flame.

Finally defeat it with their roaring laughter
and helmets on floor and armchair, drinking beer
like an advertisement for a brand name — 'after the fire
the dark blue conqueror relaxes here'
in an abandonment of blue and gold
that Rousseau the Douanier might have set
meticulously upon a canvas — those red brick
faces, vacant, those bright axes
and the weltering dark serge angles of arms and legs.

So they attacked their fire and put it out.
No tendril of silence grew in the green room when they went
into the night like night with only the six

stars of their helmets shining omnipotent
in a fiery constellation
pinking the darkness with a sign unknown
to ride the street like a flume, to fan to flame
smouldering branches of artery and vein
in beautiful conflagration, their lovely dream.

PUPPETS

See them joined by strings to history:
their strange progenitors all born full-grown,
ancestors buried with the ancient Greeks —
slim terra-cotta dolls with articulate limbs
lying like corpses.
                                    Puppets in Rome
subject to papal law, discreet in tights.

And see the types perpetuate themselves
freed from the picket prejudice of race:
the seaside Punch with his inherited nose
carried from Pulcinella round the globe
ends up in Bexhill, enters English eyes.

While here in a Sunday drawing-room beside
the bland Pacific and its rain come two
emerging full-grown from their dark cocoons —
two whose blasé antecedents once
performed for Pepys's mistress, or, in silk,
were bawdy for bored royalty at court;
escaped and raided country fairs and spread
the world with areas of Lilliput.

Before our eyes the twelve inch clown grows large
and dances on his rubber feet and kicks
pneumatic legs, thumbs his enormous nose;
lies down for push-ups — and, exhibitionist —
suddenly turns and waves.
More clown than clowns he is all laughter, is
bouyed by it and brilliant in its light.
Unlike his living prototype has no
dichotomy to split him: this is all.
He calls your laughter out without reserve —

is only and always feet and a vulgar streak
and his music, brass.

The negro does a tap dance and his toes
click on the parquet.
Music moves in him and explodes in his toes
and somehow he is two-fold, though he grins
his hands are stripped of humour,
they are long
and lonely attached to him.

He is himself and his own symbol,
sings
terribly without a voice, is so
gentle it seems that his six delicate strings
are ropes upon him.
But still he grins, he grins.

Oh, coming isolated from their plays but not
isolated from their history,
shaped and moulded by heredity,
negro and clown in microcosm, these
small violent people shake the quiet room
and bring all history tumbling about
a giant audience that almost weeps.

MAN WITH ONE SMALL HAND

One hand is smaller than the other. It
must always be loved a little like a child;
requires attention constantly, implies
it needs his frequent glance to nurture it.

He holds it sometimes with the larger one
as adults lead a child across the street.
Finding it his or suddenly alien
rallies his interest and his sympathy.

Sometimes you come upon him unawares
just quietly staring at it where it lies
as mute and somehow perfect as a flower.

But no. It is not perfect. He admits
it has its faults: it is not strong or quick.
At night it vanishes to reappear
in dreams full-size, lost or surrealist.

Yet has its place like memory or a dog —
is never completely out of mind — a rod
to measure all uncertainties against.

Perhaps he loves it too much, sets too much stock
simply in its existence. Ah, but look!
It has its magic. See how it will fit
so sweetly, sweetly in the infant's glove.

FREAK

His plaster face he built as an armour,
in hands, the nerve ends nursed, and words
sieved through a fine muslin;
but never anonymous,
no, never nondescript
nor simply himself.
Always his monster.

His business: being a ten cent joke
a treat or terror for the kids;
beast in a marvellous cage, hanging his head
or moving his terribly funny feathery hands.
His rages, sudden and uncontrolled, bring down the house.

On big days more
popular than the tatooed lady or the giant
he feels his gift twist in his heart like a smile,
that ounce of professional pride — his glorious Christ.
And the barker a friend
and the public his personal picnic.

But away from the tent
on a holiday, not on show
everything is new
everywhere he looks, everywhere, everyone he sees
is glinting like brass
and he in their mirrors shining and bright;
locked in their light,
trapped in their pupils and pockets
and many as money.

Anounced! His name,
those letters and that sound

tapped, rung out,
repeated in rain in wheels
in the wail of wind
or yelled from nowhere —
carefully spelled by an acre of empty air.

A million reflections and his heart in each
a million names called and each one his,
falling like blows on his plaster face.

He sees the cage a fine and friendly place.

IMAGES OF ANGELS

Imagine them as they were first conceived:
part musical instrument and part daisy
in a white manshape.
Imagine a crowd on the Elysian grass
playing ring-around-a-rosy,
mute except for their singing,
their gold smiles
gold sickle moons in the white sky of their faces.
Sex, neither male nor female,
name and race, in each case, simply angel.

Who, because they are white and gold, has made them holy
but never to be loved or petted, never to be friended?

Not children, who imagine them more simply,
see them more coloured and a deal more cosy,
yet somehow mixed with the father, fearful and fully
realized when the vanishing bed
floats in the darkness,
when the shifting point of focus, that drifting star,
has settled in the head.

More easily perhaps, the little notary
who, given one as a pet, could not
walk the sun-dazzled street
with so lamb-white a companion.
For him its loom-large skeleton —
one less articulated than his own —
would dog his days with doom
until behind the lethal lock
used for his legal documents
he guiltily shut it up.
His terror then that it escape

and smiling call for him at work.
Less dreadful for his public shame
worse for his private guilt
if in the hour that he let it out
he found it limp and boneless as a flower.

Perhaps, more certainly perhaps, the financier.
What business man would buy as he buys stock
as many as could cluster on a pin?
Angels are dropping, angels going up.
He could not mouth such phrases and chagrin
would sugar round his lips as he said "angel".
For though he mocks their mention he cannot
tie their tinsel image to a tree
without the momentary lowering of his lids
for fear that they exist in worlds which he
uneasy, reconstructs from childhood's memory.

The anthropologist with his tidy science
had he stumbled upon one unawares,
found as he finds an arrowhead, an angel —
a what-of-a-thing
as primitive as a daisy,
might with his ice cold eye have assessed it coolly.
But how, despite his detailed observations
could he face his learned society and explain?
"Gentlemen, it is thought that they are born
with harps and haloes
as the unicorn with its horn.
Study discloses them white and gold as daisies."

Perhaps only a dog could accept them wholly,
be happy to follow at their heels
and bark and romp with them in the green fields.

Or, take the nudes of Lawrence and impose
a-sexuality upon them; those
could meet with ease these gilded albinos.

Or a child, not knowing they were angels could
wander along an avenue hand in hand
with his new milk-white playmates,
take a step
and all the telephone wires would become taut
as the high strings of a harp
and space be merely the spaces between strings
and the world mute, except for a thin singing,
as if a sphere — big enough to be in it
and yet small
so that a glance through the lashes
would show it whole —
were fashioned very finely out of wire
and turning in a wind.

But say the angelic word
and *this* innocent
with his almost-unicorn
would let it go —
(even a child would know
that angels should be flying in the sky!)
and feeling implicated in a lie,
his flesh would grow
cold
and snow
would cover the warm and sunny avenue.

III

PERSONAL LANDSCAPE

Where the bog ends, there, where the ground lips, lovely
is love, not lonely.
                              Land is
love, round with it, where the hand is;
wide with love, cleared scrubland, grain
on a coin.
Oh, the wheat-field, the rock-bound rubble;
the untouched hills
                              as a thigh smooth;
the meadow.
Not only the poor soil lovely, the outworn prairie,
but the green upspringing,
the lark-land,
the promontory.

A lung-born land, this,
a breath spilling,
scanned by the valvular heart's
field glasses.

THE APPLE

Look, look, he took me straight
to the snake's eye
to the striped flower
shielding its peppery root.

I said, I shall never go back.

At harvest he led me round and about.
The ground
was apple red and round.
The trees bare.
One apple only hung like a heart in air.

Together, bite by bite
we ate,
mouths opposite.
Bit clean through core and all to meet:
through sweet juice met.

I said, I shall never go back.

But someone let an angel down
on a thin string.
It was a rangey paper thing
with one wing torn,
born of a child.

Now, now, we come and go, we come and go,
feverish where that harvest grew.

THE GLASS AIR

I dreamed my most extraordinary darling
gangling, come to share
my hot and prairie childhood

the first day loosed the mare from her picket
and rode her bareback
over the little foothills towards the mountains.

And on the second, striding from his tent,
twisted a noose of butcher's string.
Ingenious to my eyes the knots he tied.

The third bright day he laid the slack noose over
the gopher's burrow,
unhurried by the chase,

and lolled a full week, lazy, in the sun
until the head popped, sleek, enquiring.
The noose pulled tight around its throat.

Then the small fur lashed, lit out, hurling
about only to turn
tame silk in his palm

as privy harness, tangled from his pocket
with leash of string
slipped simply on.

But the toy beast and the long rein and the paid out lengths
of our youth snapped
as the creature jibbed and bit

and the bright blood ran out, the bright blood trickled over,
slowed, grew dark
lay sticky on our skins.

And we two, dots upon that endless plain, Leviathan became
and filled and broke
the glass air like twin figures, vast, in stone.

FAILURE AT TEA

The table was too wide
and surely it was a quarter shedding the flat light
that made us two-dimensional.
Over the cups
yesterday's waitress wore her welcome hands,
failed and was finished,
leaned against a wall.
Somebody at a silent table sang
and in our acre you and I were lost.

Plates rattled somewhere in the porcelain ear
and vicious as a drug our words became
quick nickels pushed in broken slot machines.
No jackpot rang,
no Petty blonde undressed,
the little guy who should have made a goal
stood as he was —
inanimate under glass.

Walking between the tables to the desk
nobody cried or waved —
as if a train
pulled from an empty station in the night.

But it was daylight.
In the boughs of trees
space hung about like washing.
Through the snow
faces went by like flags before a fear.

Standing as twins, in bas relief, I knew
neon illuminate
the printless news:
our failure even was not ours alone.

THE FLOWER AND THE ROCK

She felt the flower of his pain beneath her hand
which cupped for it and was soft and yearned as if
all her blood had withdrawn to the stamping wrist
and her hand was wax, wanting the pain in it
so that it came, incised and exquisite
as the fossil of fern or a delicate hairy plant
which almost lived, almost uncurled and bloomed
perishably and purely in her palm.

While he felt only the solid rock of pain
crack to receive the violence of the sword
whenever she came or asked or said his name.

WATER AND MARBLE

And shall I tell him that the thought of him
turns me to water
and when his name is spoken pale still sky
trembles and breaks and moves like blowing water
that winter thaws its frozen drifts in water
all matter blurs, unsteady, seen through water
and I, in him, dislimn, water in water?

As true: the thought of him
has made me marble
and when his name is spoken blowing sky
settles and freezes in a dome of marble
and winter seals its floury drifts in marble
all matter double-locks as dense as marble
and I, in other's eyes, am cut from marble.

THE METAL AND THE FLOWER

Intractable between them grows
a garden of barbed wire and roses.
Burning briars like flames devour
their too innocent attire.
Dare they meet, the blackened wire
tears the intervening air.

Trespassers have wandered through
texture of flesh and petals.
Dogs like arrows moved along
pathways that their noses knew.
While the two who laid it out
find the metal and the flower
fatal underfoot.

Black and white at midnight glows
this garden of barbed wire and roses.
Doused with darkness roses burn
coolly as a rainy moon;
beneath a rainy moon or none
silver the sheath on barb and thorn.

Change the garden, scale and plan:
wall it, make it annual.
There the briary flower grew.
There the brambled wire ran.
While they sleep the garden grows,
deepest wish annuls the will:
perfect still the wire and rose.

PHOTOGRAPH

They are all beneath the sea in this photograph —
not dead surely — merely a little muted:
those two lovers lying apart and stiff
with a buoy above which could ring their beautiful
      movements;

and she with the book, reading as through a bowl
words that were never written, f's like giraffes
and vowels distorted and difficult as code
which make her lazily turn away and laugh;

he with hands so pale they might be dying
sits with paints and paper painting sand
and wears a skin of corrugated water
which stillness opens on his sea-scape mind.

And all their paraphernalia a pretense:
cigarettes, matches, cameras and dark glasses
and the pair of water wings which refuse to float
are idle in their submarine oasis.

While overhead the swimmers level waves,
shrinking the distance between continents
and closer inland from the broken wiers
the fishermen are hauling giant nets.

CROSS

He has leaned for hours against the veranda railing
gazing the darkened garden out of mind
while she with battened hatches rides out the wind
that will blow for a year or a day, there is no telling.

As to why they are cross she barely remembers now.
That they *are* cross, she is certain. They hardly speak.
Feel cold and hurt and stoney. For a week
have without understanding behaved so.

And will continue so to behave for neither
can come to that undemanded act of love —
kiss the sleeping princess or sleep with the frog —
and break the spell which holds them each from the other.

Or if one ventures towards it, the other, shy
dissembles, regrets too late the dissimulation
and sits hands slack, heart tiny, the hard solution
having again passed by.

Silly the pair of them. Yet they make me weep.
Two on a desert island, back to back
who, while the alien world howls round them black
go their own ways, fall emptily off to sleep.

MINERAL

Soft and unmuscular among the flowers and papers
and changed as if grown deaf or slightly lame
she writes to strangers about him as if he were a stranger,
avoids the name
which he no longer has a use for, which
he disinherited as he was leaving.
It had a different ring when he was living.

Now he is mineral to her. In a game
she would declare him mineral without thinking.
Mineral his going and his having gone
and on her desk, his photo — mineral.

No gentle mirage loves her as a dream
can love a person's head, no memory
comes warm and willing to her tears. She walks
nearly begonia between the walls,
calls out against an echo. Nothing's real
but mineral: cold touch, sharp taste of it
lodger forever in her routed house.

CONTAGION

Beside these streams, by wet and open lakes
where weeping willows, stripped of their leaves, are fountains —
singly or in faded pairs they walk
the twisted paths beneath the dripping trees
almost as if their mouths were sealed and words
forced to parade as ghosts.

Those who have suffered from the same disease
can spot them in a minute — it's as though
they're recent exiles from a fever who,
compelled by echo,
search for the lost peaks of delirium's mountains
in a land where temperatures are low.

And re-infected by their look and by
the flat horizon and the weeping trees,
now if my lover were to come like a lion
over the muted grasses, even I
would view him for a moment with their eyes,
feel locked outside the currents he released.

LOVE POEM

Remembering you and reviewing
our structural love
the past re-arises alive
from its smothering dust.

For memory which is only decadent
in hands like a miser's
loving the thing for its thingness,
or in the eyes of collectors who assess
the size, the incredible size, of their collection,
can, in the living head, create and make
new the sometimes appallingly ancient present
and sting the sleeping thing
to a sudden seeing.

And as a tree with all its leaves relaxed
shivers at the memory of wind
or the still waters of a pool recall
their springing origin and rise and fall
suddenly over the encircling basin's lip —
so I, remembering from now to then
can know and see and feel again, as jewels
must when held in a brilliant branch of sun.

T-BAR

Relentless, black on white, the cable runs
through metal arches up the mountain side.
At intervals giant pickaxes are hung
on long hydraulic springs. The skiers ride
propped by the axehead, twin automatons
supported by its handle, one each side.

In twos they move slow motion up the steep
incision in the mountain. Climb. Climb.
Somnambulists, bolt upright in their sleep
their phantom poles swung lazily behind,
while to the right, the empty T-bars keep
in mute descent, slow monstrous jigging time.

Captive the skiers now and innocent,
wards of eternity, each pair alone.
They mount the easy vertical ascent,
pass through successive arches, bride and groom,
as through successive naves, are newly wed
participants in some recurring dream.

So do they move forever. Clocks are broken.
In zones of silence they grow tall and slow,
inanimate dreamers, mild and gentle-spoken
blood-brothers of the haemophilic snow
until the summit breaks and they awaken
imagos from the stricture of the tow.

Jerked from her chrysalis the sleeping bride
suffers too sudden freedom like a pain.
The dreaming bridegroom severed from her side
singles her out, the old wound aches again.
Uncertain, lost, upon a wintry height
these two, not separate, but no longer one.

Now clocks begin to peck and sing. The slow
extended minute like a rubber band
contracts to catapult them through the snow
in tandem trajectory while behind
etching the sky-line, obdurate and slow
the spastic T-bars pivot and descend.

PHOTOS OF A SALT MINE

How innocent their lives look,
how like a child's
dream of caves and winter, both combined;
the steep descent to whiteness
and the stope
with its striated walls
their folds all leaning as if pointing to
the greater whiteness still,
that great white bank
with its decisive front,
that seam upon a slope,
salt's lovely ice.

And wonderful underfoot the snow of salt
the fine
particles a broom could sweep,
one thinks
muckers might make angels in its drifts
as children do in snow,
lovers in sheets,
lie down and leave imprinted where they lay
a feathered creature holier than they.

And in the outworked stopes
with lamps and ropes
up miniature matterhorns
the miners climb
probe with their lights
the ancient folds of rock —
syncline and anticline —
and scoop from darkness an Aladdin's cave:
rubies and opals glitter from its walls.

But hoses douse the brilliance of these jewels,

melt fire to brine.
Salt's bitter water trickles thin and forms,
slow fathoms down,
a lake within a cave,
lacquered with jet —
white's opposite.
There grey on black the boating miners float
to mend the stays and struts of that old stope
and deeply underground
their words resound,
are multiplied by echo, swell and grow
and make a climate of a miner's voice.

So all the photographs like children's wishes
are filled with caves or winter,
innocence
has acted as a filter,
selected only beauty from the mine.
Except in the last picture,
it is shot
from an acute high angle. In a pit
figures the size of pins are strangely lit
and might be dancing but you know they're not.
Like Dante's vision of the nether hell
men struggle with the bright cold fires of salt,
locked in the black inferno of the rock:
the filter here, not innocence but guilt.

Ancient nomadic snowman has rolled round.
His spoor: a wide swathe on the white ground
signs of a wintry struggle where he stands.

Stands? Yes, he stands. What snowman sat?
Legless, indeed, but more as if he had
legs than had not.

White double O, white nothing nothing, this
the child's first man on a white paper, his
earliest and fistful image is

now three-dimensional. Abstract. Everyman.
Of almost manna, he is still no man
no person, this so personal snowman.

O transient un-inhabitant, I know
no child who, on seeing the leprous thaw
undo your whitened torso and face of snow

would not, had he the magic
call you back
from that invisible attack

even knowing he can, with the new miracle
of another and softer and whiter snowfall
make you again, this time more wonderful.

SNOWMAN

Innocent single snowman. Overnight
brings him — a bright
omen — a thunderbolt of white.

But once I saw a mute in every yard
come like a plague; a stock-still multitude
and all stone-buttoned, bun-faced and absurd.

And next day they were still there but each
had changed a little as if all had inched
forward or back, I barely knew which;

and greyed a little too, grown sinister
and disreputable in their sooty fur,
numb, unmoving and nothing moving near.

And as far as I could see the snow was scarred
only with angels' wing marks or the feet of birds
like twigs broken upon the snow or shards

discarded. And I could hear no sound
as far as I could hear except a round
kind of an echo without end

rung like a hoop below them and above
jarring the air they had no need of
in a landscape without love.

VEGETABLE ISLAND

Flowers own it.
Everywhere their flags flutter.
The deep woods are stormed
and trees throw bouquets to each other, pass
petals along from bough to bough.
It is theirs.

There is no window they have not invaded,
pressed or crept over the sill of, flung
their scent like a symbol through an entire room.
Business men in offices, dictating,
smelling the hanging baskets from the streets
stop and wonder about their gardens, ponder
are they too lush and lovely lovely are they
a little out of hand? The hedges calling
coyly as they advance,
the bright grass
silently leaping.

Sometimes a man must seek the sea out here.
Down where small lichens stucco all the rocks
it smacks with a smell of chowder on the shore.
A cormorant with periscope neck floats black
among the gulls. Some bird in tiny ambush stamps about,
undoes the sudden buzzer in its throat,
and breaks the sweetness of the simmering gorse.
Oh, undiseased by pollen, hand in water
beneath the saline wave is sharp and clear
unsmudged by pastel petal, uncorrupted.

Sometimes a man must strip and throw his body
into the acid ocean to erase
the touch and scent of flowers, their little cries
like sickly mistresses, their gentle faces

pleading consumption.
Sometimes he has no strength to meet a tree
debauched with blossoms.

But women wander unafraid as if
they made the petals
and tiny children in the meadows wave
with wildflowers in their fists
or strip the woods of flowers
and turn away
to fresh and unrelated interests
as if the flesh were only hurt by what
is made of metal — knife-blade or buckshot.

STORIES OF SNOW

Those in the vegetable rain retain
an area behind their sprouting eyes
held soft and rounded with the dream of snow
precious and reminiscent as those globes —
souvenir of some never-nether land —
which hold their snow-storms circular, complete,
high in a tall and teakwood cabinet.

In countries where the leaves are large as hands
where flowers protrude their fleshy chins
and call their colours,
an imaginary snow-storm sometimes falls
among the lilies.
And in the early morning one will waken
to think the glowing linen of his pillow
a northern drift, will find himself mistaken
and lie back weeping.
And there the story shifts from head to head,
of how in Holland, from their feather beds
hunters arise and part the flakes and go
forth to the frozen lakes in search of swans —
the snow-light falling white along their guns,
their breath in plumes.
While tethered in the wind like sleeping gulls
ice-boats wait the raising of their wings
to skim the electric ice at such a speed
they leap jet strips of naked water,
and how these flying, sailing hunters feel
air in their mouths as terrible as ether.
And on the story runs that even drinks
in that white landscape dare to be no colour;
how flasked and water clear, the liquor slips
silver against the hunters' moving hips.
And of the swan in death these dreamers tell

of its last flight and how it falls, a plummet,
pierced by the freezing bullet
and how three feathers, loosened by the shot,
descend like snow upon it.
While hunters plunge their fingers in its down
deep as a drift, and dive their hands
up to the neck of the wrist
in that warm metamorphosis of snow
as gentle as the sort that woodsmen know
who, lost in the white circle, fall at last
and dream their way to death.

And stories of this kind are often told
in countries where great flowers bar the roads
with reds and blues which seal the route to snow —
as if, in telling, raconteurs unlock
the colour with its complement and go
through to the area behind the eyes
where silent, unrefractive whiteness lies.

SLEEPER

The ritual of bedtime takes its shape
meadowed with sheets and hilled with pillows plumped
for head's indenture —
oh, the prairie air's plangent with scent of soap.

Now, silken, smooth, the body stretches out
easy with sleep;
beneath the lazy hand
print that the eye has sprinted on grows fur
to stroke a milky eye.

Light goes with an explosion.
In the head
colours remain like ribbons —
drift and blow;
move and are static, fill a floating frame,
flow over and reform in fern and sand.

The gentle dreamer drowns without a sound
softly in eiderdown.
Almost, he dies.
As divers who are dead, his body floats
pneumatic on black tides.

Complete in sleep, discards his arms and legs
with only whimpers;
from his flesh retreats
like water through a mesh, leaving it beached
alone upon a bed.

And takes the whole night in his lungs and head.
A hydrocephalic idiot, quick at sums
wandering strangely lost and loose among
symbols as blunted and as bright as flowers.

IF IT WERE YOU

If it were you, say, you
who scanning the personal map one day knew
your sharp eyes water and grow colour blind,
unable to distinguish green from blue
and everything terribly run together as if rain
had smudged the markings on the paper —
a child's painting after a storm —
and the broad avenue erased,
the landmarks gone;
and you, bewildered — not me this time and not
the cold unfriendly neighbour or the face in the news —
who walked a blind circle in a personal place;

and if you became lost, say, on the lawn,
unable to distinguish left from right
and that strange longitude that divides the body
sharply in half — that line that separates
so that one hand could never be the other —
dissolved and both your hands were one,
then in the garden though birds went on with their
                    singing
and on the ground
flowers wrote their signatures in coloured ink —
would you call help like a woman assaulted,
cry to be found?

No ears would understand. Your friends and you
would be practically strangers, there would be no face
more familiar than this unfamiliar place
and there would be walls of air, invisible, holding
you single and directionless in space.

First you would be busy as a woodsman marking
the route out, making false starts and then

remembering yesterday when it was easy
you would grow lazy.
Summer would sit upon you then as on a stone
and you would be tense for a time beneath the morning sun
but always lonely
and birds perhaps would brush your coat and become
angels of deliverance
for a moment only;
clutching their promising wings you would discover
they were illusive and gone
as the lost lover.
Would you call Ariel, Ariel, in the garden,
in a dream within a dream be Orpheus
and for a certain minute take a step
delicately across the grass?

If so, there would be no answer nor reply
and not one coming forward from the leaves.
No bird nor beast with a challenging look
or friendly.
Simply nothing but you and the green garden,
you and the garden.

And there you might stay forever, mechanically
occupied, but if you raised your head
madness would rush at you from the shrubbery
or the great sun, stampeding through the sky
would stop and drop —
a football in your hands
and shrink as you watched it
to a small dark dot
forever escaping focus
like the injury to the cornea which darts
hard as a cinder across the sight but dims

fading into the air like a hocus-pocus
the minute that you are aware
and stare at it.

Might you not, if it were you,
bewildered, broken,
slash your own wrists, commit
an untidy murder in the leafy lane

and scar the delicate air with your cries or sit
weeping, weeping in the public square
your flimsy butterfly fingers in your hair
your face destroyed by rain?

If it were you, the person you call "I,"
the one you loved and worked for,
the most high
now become Ishmael,
might you not
grow phobias about calendars and clocks,
stare at your face in the mirror, not knowing it
and feel an identity with idiots and dogs
as all the exquisite unborns of your dreams
deserted you to snigger behind their hands?

THE SICK

All these, the horizontal and inactive,
held in the fronds of fever
or crooks of pain,
with their many-pupilled and respective
eyes floating like water flowers on a stagnant river
or tight and walled as stone,
inhabit a country that is all their own.

Lie on the personal white plains of beds
but not as sleepers do,
giving themselves,
nor yet as lovers, windmills in their heads;
but emptied out as hoof-prints where the cattle go,
they live, pathetic halves,
pallidly hoping to complete themselves.

Some in the levitation of half sleep
with heads like dandelions
seeded and soft
have lost their bodies as they lost their hopes
and float like freaks in air — pneumatic scions —
inflated by a cough
to altitudes where there is nothing left.

Others as white as nurses, clean as soap,
drift in a scent of pink
with roses nudging them
into a patent and elastic sleep
where they can soar with suns before they sink
below the nurses' hems
single and cool and fresh as roses' stems.

While all the others in the coal hole dark,
lighting their own despair

and unattended
except by bills and fears about their work
are pale as oysters when exposed to air
and illness ended,
the thing that's broken in them is not mended.

For loneliness and fear signal like scouts
in jumping semaphore
from head to heart,
or joined, light flares and never put them out
and from the dying ones, set fire to more;
so, single as a dart
the body is; as single as a dart

and yet is multiple, rubs shoulders with
twins at each corner
shakes its own hands
while meeting foreigners and living myths
and rarely knows itself to be the owner
of common dividends
through having interest in a hundred lands.

THE SENTIMENTAL SURGEON

Watch him perform — the sentimental surgeon —
anaesthetize with scent
the dying patient,
hide raw hand in the pastel glove.
Diagnosis proclaims the operation urgent,
yet flowers float sadly in his salon face
where tense and straining at their tendon traces
should crouch the whippets of love.

Sickle of students swings and is suspended,
sees his evasion
to make the incision,
sees fruit knife whetted on the strop of sleeve;
knowing that already the lesson is ended,
the promise — a pastiche of sound and scent
mixed with a tray of useless instruments —
the sickle breaks and leaves.

Ready at last, the square of flesh exposed,
he holds the smiling knife,
and lean with grief,
draws an artistic line upon the patient;
reflexes curl the clusters of his toes,
he turns away and suffers — plucked, his eyes,
the petals saying "no-yes-no," he cries
in the enamel basin.

Nurse who is pledged to serve and make no sound
is standing by with sponge
while her rebellious lungs
are bright with anger and her molten lips
welded. He whispers to the wound;
softly, as butter melts, he operates —

taps, pats and probes; when faced with fact escapes
through flabby nerves and pitying fingertips.

Sutures, relieved, with lazy-daisy stitch,
is pleased and smiles
as when a child
he made a needle case for his frail mother;
checks the desire to finish with a kiss
and weeping sees the supine body rolled
backward to poison and infect a world
as it unwraps from ether.

* * *

The ailing patient wears away the bed.
Not being healed
or adequately killed
death pangs and life are dangerously convergent.
Asleep he puts the bell beneath his head,
awake he watches with some extra eye
the mountains of his health's geography
and waits the daily visit of his surgeon.

PROBATIONER

Floats out of anaesthetic
helium-hipped
a bird a bride your breath could bruise,
is blurred.

Re-forms in bright enamel, tiny, chips
into recurring selves
a hundred of her
giving you smiles and small white pills of water.

Grows in delirium as striped and strange
as any tiger crouching in the flowers.
Her metal finger tip
taps out your pulse.

Intrinsic to your pain
lives in its acre —
is only there because your wound has made her.
Beyond its radius she has never been.

Is sly and clever suddenly, creates
you wholly out of sheets and air — full-grown.
Most wonderfully makes a halo of your hair.
Gives you a name: your own.

Or in the easy mornings comes with smiles,
tipping the window so it spills the sun
carries the basin plastic with slipping water
and calls it fun.

For she is only a girl and crisis over
she is herself again — clumsy and gauche,
her jokes too hearty
and her touch too rough.

And by a slow dissolve
becomes at last,
someone you've always known —
yourself perhaps.

Yet alters when you leave. From her stiff starch
she overflows in laughs, is proud and shy
and as if you are a present she has made,
she gives you away.

NURSING HOME

Old women will not enter paradise. They will be made young and beautiful first.

Mahomet.

Where have they gone
the inhabitants of these bodies?

(I think of hermit crabs'
dry jerking passage over shifting beaches)

Tennis champions
barely able to move
ancient scholars
mindless as newts
pulling themselves along
with sticks and handrails
moving decrepit
directionless
in wheel chairs
stopping without reason
reasoning with
demonic
private logic

Old men, old women
Which are which?
Trembling, teetering, dribbling, calling

Some still peer out through their eyes
The sharpened points of their gaze
engage me, probe

One sings unending Jingle Bells

Their failing strengths
surge in monstrous energies:
'NURSE   HELP'
barked like a dog
'My father will see you are
amply rewarded'
'TAKE   ME   OUT'

Who yelled?
What mouth
allowed that metal out?

They sit like parsnips
boiled potatoes
propped, inert
Do they feel vegetable?
Mineral?
Cold stone
dense slumbering stone?
Pellets of lead?

Sedatives mineralize
Even the nurses
are white and obdurate
as onyx

> (I know this place
> this gray and mineral kingdom
> its mineral animals
> its static hours
> I have been trapped
> in a dying mineral
> my half life had more digits

than I could count
myself mineral
muted, caught
in mineral immensities
the vegetation as enduring
as plastic flowers)

There are no words for it
there are no words

'I am Josephine Maria Plumtree
killed a dog
That's my identity
You take a saw — a little saw
and cut away the jaw
Josephine Maria Plumtree
killed a dog'

'NURSE   HELP
I want a knife to cut these strings'

Where are they going
these voyagers?

Who steers?

ELEMENT

Feeling my face has the terrible shine of fish
caught and swung on a line under the sun
I am frightened held in the light that people make
and sink in darkness freed and whole again
as fish returned by dream into the stream.

Oh running water is not rough; ruffled to eye,
to flesh it is flat and smooth; to fish
silken as children's hands in milk.

I am not wishful in this dream of immersion.
Mouth becomes full with darkness
and the shine, mottled and pastel, sounds its own note, not
the fake high treble thrown on resounding faces.

There are flowers — and this is pretty for the summer —
light on the bed of darkness;
there are stones that glisten and grow slime;
winters that question nothing, are a new
night for the passing movement of fine fins;
and quietly, by the reeds or water fronds
something can cry without discovery.

Ah in daylight the shine is single
as dime flipped or gull on fire or fish
silently hurt — its mouth alive with metal.

ARRAS

Consider a new habit — classical,
and trees espaliered on the wall like candelabra.
How still upon that lawn our sandalled feet.

But a peacock rattling his rattan tail and screaming
has found a point of entry. Through whose eye
did it insinuate in furled disguise
to shake its jewels and silk upon that grass?

The peaches hang like lanterns. No one joins
those figures on the arras.
                              Who am I
or who am I become that walking here
I am observer, other, Gemini,
starred for a green garden of cinema?

I ask, what did they deal me in this pack?
The cards, all suits, are royal when I look.
My fingers slipping on a monarch's face
twitch and grow slack.
I want a hand to clutch, a heart to crack.

No one is moving now, the stillness is
infinite. If I should make a break. . . .
take to my springy heels. . . . ? But nothing moves.
The spinning world is stuck upon its poles,
the stillness points a bone at me. I fear
the future on this arras.
                              I confess:

It was my eye.

Voluptuous it came.
Its head the ferrule and its lovely tail
folded so sweetly; it was strangely slim
to fit the retina. And then it shook
and was a peacock — living patina,
eye-bright, maculate!
Does no one care?

I thought their hands might hold me if I spoke.
I dreamed the bite of fingers in my flesh,
their poke smashed by an image, but they stand
as if within a treacle, motionless,
folding slow eyes on nothing. While they stare
another line has trolled the encircling air,
another bird assumes its furled disguise.

IV

NOW THIS COLD MAN . . .

Now this cold man in his garden feels the ice
thawing from branches of his lungs and brain:
the blood thins out in artery and vein,
the stiff eyes slip again.

Kneeling in welters of narcissus his
dry creaking joints bend with a dancer's ease,
the roughened skin softens beneath the rain

and all that he had clutched, held tightly locked
behind the fossil frame
dissolves, flows free
in saffron covering the willow tree
and coloured rivers of the rockery.

Yellow and white and purple is his breath
his hands are curved and cool for cupping petals,
the sharp green shoots emerging from the beds
all whistle for him

until he is the garden; heart, the sun
and all his body soil;
glistening jonquils blossom from his skull,
the bright expanse of lawn his stretching thighs
and something rare and perfect, yet unknown,
stirs like a foetus just behind his eyes.

THE PERMANENT TOURISTS

Somnolent through landscapes and by trees
nondescript, almost anonymous,
they alter as they enter foreign cities —
the terrible tourists with their empty eyes
longing to be filled with monuments.

Verge upon statues in the public squares
remembering the promise of memorials
yet never enter the entire event
as dogs, abroad in any kind of weather,
move perfectly within their rainy climate.

Lock themselves into snapshots on the steps
of monolithic bronze as if suspecting
the subtle mourning of the photograph
might later conjure in the memory
all they are now incapable of feeling.

And search all heroes out: the boy who gave
his life to save a town; the stolid queen;
forgotten politicians minus names
and the plunging war dead, permanently brave,
forever and ever going down to death.

Look, you can see them nude in any café
reading their histories from the bill of fare,
creating futures from a foreign teacup.
Philosophies like ferns bloom from the fable
that travel is broadening at the café table.

Yet somehow beautiful, they stamp the plaza.
Classic in their anxiety they call
all sculptured immemorial stone
into their passive eyes, as rivers
draw ruined columns to their placid glass.

BRAZILIAN HOUSE

In this great house white
as a public urinal
I pass my echoing days.
Only the elephant ear leaves
listen outside my window
to the tap of my heels.

Downstairs the laundress
with elephantiasis
sings like an angel
her brown wrists cuffed with suds
and the skinny little black girl
polishing silver laughs to see
her face appear in a tray.

Ricardo, stealthy
lowers his sweating body
into the stream
my car will cross when I
forced by the white porcelain
yammering silence drive
into the hot gold gong
of noon day.

BRAZILIAN FAZENDA

That day all the slaves were freed
their manacles, anklets
left on the window ledge to rust in the moist air

and all the coffee ripened
like beads on a bush or balls of fire
as merry as Christmas

and the cows all calved and the calves all lived
such a moo.

On the wide verandah where birds in cages
sang among the bell flowers
I in a bridal hammock
white and tasselled
whistled

and bits fell out of the sky near Nossa Senhora
who had walked all the way in bare feet from Bahia

and the chapel was lit by a child's
fistful of marigolds on the red velvet altar
thrown like a golden ball.

Oh let me come back on a day
when nothing extraordinary happens
so I can stare
at the sugar white pillars
and black lace grills
of this pink house.

COOK'S MOUNTAINS

By naming them he made them.
They were there
before he came
but they were not the same.
It was his gaze
that glazed each one.
He saw
the Glass House Mountains in his glass.
They shone.

And still they shine.
We saw them as we drove —
sudden, surrealist, conical
they rose
out of the rain forest.
The driver said,
"Those are the Glass House Mountains up ahead."

And instantly they altered to become
the sum of shape and name.
Two strangenesses united into one
more strange than either.
Neither of us now
remembers how they looked before they broke
the light to fragments as the driver spoke.

Like mounds of mica,
hive-shaped hothouses,
mountains of mirror glimmering
they form
in diamond panes behind the tree ferns of

the dark imagination,
burn and shake
the lovely light of Queensland like a bell
reflecting Cook upon a deck
his tongue
silvered with paradox and metaphor.

STORM IN MEXICO

Sky blackening that day over badlands.
Red badlands. Sky blackening, rolling, finally falling.
Rivers of blood cutting wide earth wide open.
Indios out of nowhere in straw raincoats
looking like cornsheaves. Hauling black donkeys.

Our car from another age. Hermetic. Metal.
And rain running on the cornsheaf coats of *los indios*.
Soaking their donkeys. Dissolving their maize plots.
Drumming our hardtop. Our skins dry.
Our hearts uneducated.

JOURNEY HOME

Certainly there had been nothing but the extraordinary rain for
                                                    a long time —
nothing but the rain, the grey buildings, the grey snow,
when landscape broke the lens and smacked his face
with a flag of blue
and the white thunder of snow
rolling the hills.

Hurry was in his veins;
violence vaulted the loose-box of his head;
hurry was hot in the straw
and snapped in the eyes
of the innocent traveller.

And flex and flux were there
like acrobats
waving their banners.
So declamatory was his blood
that he owned the train;
its whistle was in his throat,
its wheels in his brain.

Once he became a panoramic view,
the white of the valleys and hills
his own still flesh.
But speed re-formed him
he was forced to change
his contours and his outlook and his range.
Rushing through forest he was dark again
and the great coniferous branches brushed his face.

Rabbit spoor resembled his memory
of what he once had been — faint against faintness,
definite as dust,

of the no-taste of wafers, of the warmth
that neither gives nor takes.
Past was a pastel rubbed as he hurried past.

And now that the tunnel of trees was done, his eyes
sprinted the plain where house lights in the dusk
fired pistols for the race that led him on.
He shed the train like a snake its skin; he dodged
the waiting camera which with a simple click
could hold him fast to the spot beside the track.

And as the air inflated his lungs he stood
there in the dark at his destination knowing
somewhere — to left? to right? — he was walking home
and his shoulders were light and white as though wings were
                                              growing.

CHRISTMAS EVE — MARKET SQUARE

City of Christmas, here, I love your season,
where in the market square,
bristled and furry
like a huge animal
the fir trees lie
silently waiting buyers.
>   It's as if
>   they hold the secrets of a Christmas sealed —
>   as statues hold their feelings sealed in stone —
>   to burst in bells and baubles on their own
>   within the warmth and lightness of a house.

The sellers, bunched and bundled,
hold their ears,
blow lazy boas as they call their wares,
and children out of legends pulling sleds,
prop tall trees straight in search of symmetry
and haul their spikey aromatic wonder
home through a snowy world.
>   Almost the tree sings through them in their carols
>   almost grows taller in their torsos, is
>   perfectly theirs, as nothing ever was.

The soft snow falls,
vague smiling drunkards weave
gently as angels through a street of feathers;
balancing bulging parcels with their wings
they tip-toe where the furry monster grows
smaller and hoarier
and nerveless sprawls
flat on its mammoth, unimagined face.
>   While in far separate houses
>   all its nerves

spring up like rockets,
unknown children see
a miracle
and cry
to cut the ceiling not to lop the tree.

RAGE

How use so fine a rage?
Why waste upon bare air
so grand a water-spout?
God! let it sink a boat
and swamp an island near
where that boat did float
then whistle on and blow —
cooler now and so
merely a whim of rage —
whales in the bloody air.

TRUCE

My enemy in a purple hat
looks suddenly like a plum
and I am dumb with wonder
at the thought
of feuding with a fruit.

SHAMAN

Now to be healed of an old wound requires
diet, cautery, exercise and spells.

The shaman is solemn.
He burns herbs.
The air is moireéd, rainbowed even.
I am chilled.
In the folds of his intricate robes
of feathers, furs
beads like a bird's eyes
pale polished bone,
his curled hands lie
one upon the other, relaxed, as if asleep.
Hands curiously painted with my name and yours.

Messages are transmitted mind to mind.
For just as long as he wishes
my mind twins his.
Small images of you form and fill my head
they are leaden images and heavy as lead
weigh down my eyelids
weigh down my head
torso, arms, legs, feet.
I am a dead weight held fast to the dead.
White wires pin and bind me.
Am I asleep?

He prescribes salves and potions, uses words
from another language.
The lines of his face spell out undecipherable messages.
When he opens his lips to speak he displays a jade
green satiny lining to his mouth and throat.
Is he *Diphyllodes Magnificus* in disguise?

Tropical? Pied plumage of paradise?
I am no longer certain.
Is he man? Or bird?

It is all that twittering perhaps.
Short vowels. Long.
Quick clicking consonants.
Inscrutable eyes
bright as black currants.
Tall curious plumes
nodding as he moves.
Faint peppery whiff of dung.

THEY MIGHT HAVE BEEN ZEBRAS
(For Margaret)

They might have been zebras. I'd have been no more surprized
than to see by daylight four night raccoons, full-grown
walking bear-like in indian file across
our isthmus of bright grass
so black and white, their fur so fluffed and upright
black masked, tails ringed with black and white
utterly foreign to morning's minted light
and violent as newsprint on the viridian lawn.

It's not that they're unfamiliar. We have met
dozens of times in darkness. They've climbed and gazed
down at me from the Douglas fir's right-angled boughs —
sly and furtive watchers — or, bold and wild
hauled from our obsidian pool gold fish whose scales
in the moonlight shine like pieces of eight.
We acknowledge each other at night. We meet and stare
shadowy form at shadowy form. I chain the dog
leave offerings for them of marshmallows, raisins, bread.

But by day they immobilize me. I hold my breath.
Turn to a great soft statue with inflammable eyes
tinder for the fire they strike from the morning air.
And I see them blacker and whiter than I had dreamed
sharper, more feral, spanning the grassy isthmus
as if there might be others in front and behind —
a whole parade extending to both horizons
but hidden by the berried cotoneasters.

When they disappear I am released.
Dart through the door.
The sun is sharpening every leaf.
Its threads are spinning a golden tent.

The green is enamel or emeralds.
Petals fall more fragile than flakes of snow.
I alone, unbeautiful, in the whole morning
in flapping nightdress search every bush.
But the four who blinded me are gone.
Is this grey ash all that is left?

LEVIATHAN IN A POOL

*. . . It was a small whale, a Porpoise about eight feet long
with lovely subtle curves glistening in the cold rain. It had
been mutilated. Someone had hacked off its flukes for a
souvenir. Two other people had carved their initials deeply
into its side, and someone else had stuck a cigar butt in its
blowhole. I removed the cigar and stood there a long time
with feelings I cannot describe.*

Roger S. Payne.

Leviathan in a Pool

I

Black and white plastic
inflatable
a child's giant toy
teeth perfectly conical
tongue pink
eyes where ears are
blowhole (fontanelle
a rip in a wet inner tube
Third Eye)
out of which speech
breath
and beautiful fountains flower

So much for linear description
phrases in place of whale

This creature fills that pool
as an eye its socket
Moves   laughs like an eye
shines like an eye   eybright
eyeshaped   mandorla
of meeting worlds
forked tail attached

126

and fin
like a funny sail

It is rotund and yet
flexible as a whip
Lighter than air going up
and heavy as a truckload of bricks
It leaps sky-high   it flies
and comes down *whack*
on its freshly painted side
and the spectators get wet
drenched
soaked to the hide

Tongue lolling like a dog's
after a fast run
pleased with itself   and you
it seems to want to be petted
rears its great head up
hangs it   its tiny eyes gleam
Herring   minute as whitebait
slip down its throat
Dear whale we say as if to a child
We beam

And it disappears   Utterly
with so dark a thrust
of its muscle
through silver tines
of water
only streamers of brine
tiny tinsels of brine
remain

II

Swim round the pool vocalizing   the boy says
and *Toot* they call through their blowholes
Toot toot   Toot
At sea they will sometimes sing for thirty minutes
cadences   recognizable series of notes   songs which carry
hundreds of miles   Sing together   Sing singly

Here in a small pool they vocalize on command
joyous short toots   calls

Why am I crying?

III

Haida and Nootka respond to whistle signals
Each whistle has its own pitch
and each whale knows which is which

Haida and Nootka respond to hand signals
Fresh from the wild Pacific
they answer to hand signals

(The words are for us
who have not yet learned
that two blasts
mean

Give your trainer a big kiss
or a flick of the wrist
means   *Vocalize*)

Chimo   white as Moby
albino and still a baby

is deaf
and has poor vision
like white cats

(white men and women?)

so Chimo
cannot respond to hand or whistle

Yet this high-spirited
'lissom'
girl of a whale
unexpectedly pale
as if caught undressed
performs
She leaps like Nootka
flaps like Haida
vocalizes

What are her cues and signals?
In what realm
do her lightning actions rise?

I lean upon the pool's wet rail
Through eyes'
sightless sideways glances
seem to see
a red line on the air
as bright as blood
that threads them on one string
trainer and whales

Visitor

Look whale
earthbound airbound me
eager visitor
constant true
at your tankside

I'm the one
indistinguishable from
all your other aging fans:
inert bespectacled opaque

Where I differ
if I do
I can kick the chandelier
turn a cartwheel on the lawn

I break my barriers where I can
Challenge gravity as do you

Nootka Chimo Haida

I

Precocious   Aggressive   Skinny
Nootka took
the pool in her breach
It was hers   And Haida too
Her male
She grabbed at tourists
where they touched the rail
Was starved   Libidinous
Ate

a hundredweight
When Haida failed to
display for her
she fought
a black and white whale on fire
and flashing red
in a frenzy of skills and rages
Haida hid
Chimo developed a skin disease
lost weight

Nootka must go
Not home   Not back to sea
to its tangle of weeds
its shoals   its schools of bright
little fishes blown from glass
but swung
by crane and sling
to a waiting truck

What giant fishmonger
laid her body out
on that bed of ice?
What monstrous nurse
smeared vaseline round her blowhole
and on the bare
and drying continents of her skin?
What practised parceller
wrapped her tonnage up
in a long wet wind of sheets
so she rode the blistering air
a blimp in shrouds

lumbering down the highway
along the green
peninsula
to the winged machine?

It took tackle and hoist
to heave her up to the plane
Two fiery hours to angle her body through
the inadequate door
Four hours from the time
they had hauled her out of her pen
she was all aboard   and blind
cigar in a tube
but quick   live blubber and bone
Incredible bird

And in those four hours
"she flailed about only once"
and high and small
as a flying gull
"cried only occasionally"

II

NOVEMBER SECOND NINETEEN SEVENTY-TWO

CHIMO DEAD
OF CHEDIAK-HIGASHI SYNDROME
FOUND IN THE MORNING DEAD
BELLY UP IN THE POOL
WHITE GOLDFISH IN A BOWL
BELLY UP IN THE POOL
FOUND IN THE MORNING DEAD
OF CHEDIAK-HIGASHI SYNDROME
CHIMO DEAD

NOVEMBER SECOND NINETEEN SEVENTY-TWO

III

*We still don't know how much of Haida's
problem is physical and how much emotional.*

Thunderbolt shot
he lolls about

Refuses food
Is forcibly fed

giant egg-nogs
mega-vitamins   drugs

We all partake
of his heartbreak

Who can console
a bereaved whale?

133

Boy with a flute
plays a sweet note

Haida responds
with such sad sounds

What will restore
his lost ardor?

O wise men who look
in treatise and book

for remedy
had you thought of the sea?

AFTER RAIN

The snails have made a garden of green lace:
broderie anglaise from the cabbages,
chantilly from the choux-fleurs, tiny veils —
I see already that I lift the blind
upon a woman's wardrobe of the mind.

Such female whimsy floats about me like
a kind of tulle, a flimsy mesh,
while feet in gum boots pace the rectangles —
garden abstracted, geometry awash —
an unknown theorem argued in green ink,
dropped in the bath.
Euclid in glorious chlorophyl, half drunk.

I none too sober slipping in the mud
where rigged with guys of rain
the clothes-reel gauche
as the rangey skeleton of some
gaunt delicate spidery mute
is pitched as if
listening;
while hung from one thin rib
a silver web —
its infant, skeletal, diminutive,
now sagged with sequins, pulled ellipsoid,
glistening.

I suffer shame in all these images.
The garden is primeval, Giovanni
in soggy denim squelches by my hub
over his ruin,
shakes a doleful head.
But he so beautiful and diademmed,
his long Italian hands so wrung with rain

I find his ache exists beyond my rim
and almost weep to see a broken man
made subject to my whim.

O choir him, birds, and let him come to rest
within this beauty as one rests in love,
till pears upon the bough
encrusted with
small snails as pale as pearls
hang golden in
a heart that knows tears are a part of love.

And choir me too to keep my heart a size
larger than seeing, unseduced by each
bright glimpse of beauty striking like a bell,
so that the whole may toll,
its meaning shine
clear of the myriad images that still —
do what I will — encumber its pure line.

A BACKWARDS JOURNEY

When I was a child of say, seven
I still had serious attention to give
to everyday objects. The Dutch Cleanser —
which was the kind my mother bought —
in those days came in a round container
of yellow cardboard around which ran
the very busy Dutch Cleanser woman
her face hidden behind her bonnet
holding a yellow Dutch Cleanser can
on which a smaller Dutch Cleanser woman
was holding a smaller Dutch Cleanser can
on which a minute Dutch Cleanser woman
held an imagined Dutch Cleanser can. . . .

This was no game. The woman led me
backwards through the eye of the mind
until she was the smallest point
my thought could hold to. And at that moment
I think I knew that if no one called
and nothing broke the delicate jet
of my attention, that tiny image
could smash the atom of space and time.

THE MURDER

Trying to put an end to what is endless
trying to terminate what is outside time
is to be set upon a fruitless murder.

That body cannot die. Instead
and many years later one bright day
I found myself — dismembered, foul

in a small box. Legs, torso, arms.

Who butchered the body and put it there?
Who buried these bones, this brittle hair?

Heart — black, shrivelled — a pullet's heart.

Let air and sunlight miracle
the loathesome contents. Let the grey
bones whiten and sort themselves and beg

forgiveness for their attempted murder
of a body existing outside time
and indestructible, being endless.

YOUR HAND ONCE . . .

All crippled. All with flaws.
You, me
the wheeling young
buds blind on their stalk
eggs in their nest
sealed from sun . . .

Tuck it all up.
Turn it in.

Yet there where no flaw shows
in the full sunlight
that
bright spot, lancing sight
dancing dazzle of motes . . .
your hand once
your face
swam in that light
and shone.

MASQUERADERS

What curious masks we wear:
bald patches and grey hair
who once wore dark or fair.

Wear too much flesh or none —
a scrag of skin and bone.
The gold gone.

Bi-focalled and watch-bound
who once, time out of mind
glimpsed world without end.

Worse masquerades to come:
white cane, black gaping tomb
as if we were blind, dead, lame

who, in reality, are
dark, fair and shinier
than the masks we wear or wore.

LEATHER JACKET

One day the King laid hold on one of the peacocks and gave
orders that he should be sewn up in a leather jacket.

Suhrawardi

That peacock a prisoner
that many-eyed bird
blind.

Enclosed in a huge leather purse.
Locked in darkness.
All its pupils sealed
its tiny brain sealed
its light and fluttering heart
heavy as a plum.

Its life vegetable.
That beautiful colorful bird
a root vegetable.

Cry, cry for the peacock
hidden in heavy leather
sewn up in heavy leather
in the garden

among flowers
and flowering trees
near streams
and flowering fountains
among cicadas
and singing birds.

The peacock sees nothing
smells nothing
hears nothing at all
remembers nothing

but a terrible yearning
a hurt beyond bearing
an almost memory
of a fan of feathers
a growing garden

and sunshine falling
as light as pollen.

PREPARATION

Go out of your mind.
Prepare to go mad.
Prepare to break
split along cracks
inhabit the darks of your eyes
inhabit the whites.

Prepare to be huge.
Be prepared to be small
the least molecule
of an unlimited form.
Be a limited form
and spin in your skin
one point in its whole.

Be prepared to prepare
for what you have dreamed
to burn and be burned
to burst like a pod
to break at your seams.

Be pre-pared. And pre-pare.
But its never like that.
It is where you are not
that the fissure occurs
and the light crashes in.

CRY ARARAT!

I

In the dream the mountain near
but without sound.
A dream through binoculars
seen sharp and clear:
the leaves moving, turning
in a far wind
no ear can hear.

First soft in the distance,
blue in blue air
then sharpening, quickening
taking on green.
Swiftly the fingers
seek accurate focus
(the bird
has vanished so often
before the sharp lens
could deliver it)
then as if from the sea
the mountain appears
emerging new-washed
growing maples and firs.
The faraway, here.

Do not reach to touch it
nor labour to hear.
Return to your hand
the sense of the hand;
return to your ear
the sense of the ear.
Remember the statue,
that space in the air

which with nothing to hold
what the minute is giving
is through each point
where its marble touches air.

Then will each leaf and flower
each bird and animal
become as perfect as
the thing its name evoked
when busy as a child
the world stopped at the Word
and Flowers more real than flowers
grew vivid and immense;
and Birds more beautiful
and Leaves more intricate
flew, blew and quilted all
the quick landscape.

So flies and blows the dream
embracing like a sea
all that in it swims
when dreaming, you desire
and ask for nothing more
than stillness to receive
the I-am animal,
the We-are leaf and flower,
the distant mountain near.

II

So flies and blows the dream that haunts us when we wake
to the unreality of bright day:
the far thing almost sensed by the still skin
and then the focus lost, the mountain gone.

This is the loss that haunts our daylight hours
leaving us parched at nightfall
blowing like last year's leaves
sibilant on blossoming trees
and thirsty for the dream of the mountain
more real than any event:
more real than strangers passing on the street
in a city's architecture white as bone
or the immediate companion.

But sometimes there is one
raw with the dream of flying:
"I, a bird,
landed that very instant
and complete —
as if I had drawn a circle in my flight
and filled its shape —
find air a perfect fit.
But this my grief,
that with the next tentative lift
of my indescribable wings
the ceiling looms
heavy as a tomb.

"Must my most exquisite and private dream
remain unleavened?
Must this flipped and spinning coin that sun
could gild and make miraculous become
so swiftly pitiful?
The vision of the flight it imitates
burns brightly in my head as if a star
rushed down to touch me where I stub against
what must forever be my underground."

III

These are the dreams that haunt us,
these the fears.
Will the grey weather wake us,
toss us twice in the terrible night to tell us
the flight is cancelled
and the mountain lost?

O, then cry Ararat!

The dove believed
in her sweet wings and in the rising peak
with such a washed and easy innocence
that she found rest on land for the sole of her foot
and, silver, circled back,
a green twig in her beak.

The leaves that make the tree by day,
the green twig the dove saw fit
to lift across a world of water
break in a wave about our feet.
The bird in the thicket with his whistle
the crystal lizard in the grass
the star and shell
tassel and bell
of wild flowers blowing where we pass,
this flora-fauna flotsam, pick and touch,
requires the focus of the total I.

A single leaf can block a mountainside;
all Ararat be conjured by a leaf.

ANOTHER SPACE

Those people in a circle on the sand
are dark against its gold
turn like a wheel
revolving in a horizontal plane
whose axis — do I dream it? —
vertical
invisible
immeasurably tall
rotates a starry spool.

Yet *if* I dream
why in the name of heaven are fixed parts
within me set in motion
like a poem?

Those people in a circle reel me in.
Down the whole length of golden beach I come
willingly pulled by their rotation
slow
as a moon pulls waters
on a string
their turning circle winds around its rim.

I see them there in three dimensions yet
their height implies another space
their clothes'
surprising chiaroscuro postulates
a different spectrum.
What kaleidoscope
does air construct
that all their movements make a compass rose
surging and altering?
I speculate
on some dimension I can barely guess.

Nearer I see them dark-skinned.
They are dark. And beautiful.
Great human sunflowers spinning in a ring
cosmic as any bumble-top
the vast
procession of the planets in their dance.
And nearer still I see them — "a Chagall" —
each fiddling on an instrument — its strings
of some black woollen fibre
and its bow — feathered —
an arrow almost.
                    Arrow *is*.

For now the headman — one step forward shoots
(or does he bow or does he lift a kite
up and over the bright pale dunes of air?)
to strike the absolute centre of my skull
my absolute centre somehow
with such skill
such staggering lightness
that the blow is love.

And something in me melts.
It is as if a glass partition melts —
or something I had always thought was glass —
some pane that halved my heart
is proved, in its melting, ice.

And to-fro all the atoms pass
in bright osmosis
hitherto
in stasis locked
where now a new
direction opens like an eye.

149